Design – Deborah Goodridge

First published April 1988

ISBN 0 906520 52 5

© Middleton Press, 1988

Typeset by CitySet - Bosham 573270

Published by Middleton Press
        Easebourne Lane
        Midhurst, West Sussex
        GU29 9AZ
        ☎ *(073 081) 3169*

Printed & bound by Biddles Ltd,
        Guildford and Kings Lynn

CONTENTS

ACKNOWLEDGEMENTS

We are very grateful to the photographers mentioned in the captions for additional help so freely given. We would also like to thank Dr. & Mrs. Beckinsale, F.M. Butterfield, R. Clark, G. Croughton, D. Maasz, Mrs. D. Meeks, E. Staff, C.R. Gordon Stuart, the Editor and staff of the Witney Gazette and our wives for help given in so many different ways.

We apologise in advance for any omissions or errors in this list or the credits.

Map of pre-grouping ownerships.
(Railway Magazine)

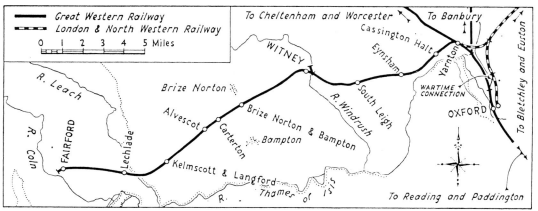

GEOGRAPHICAL SETTING

The entire route ran roughly parallel to the River Thames or Isis, crossing its many northern tributaries en route. The most notable of these is the River Windrush, which it crossed close to Witney. Here, the line was at its greatest distance from the River Thames – about five miles.

Apart from the alluvial river valley, the line was constructed mainly on Oxford Clay. The relatively flat landscape is around 200ft. above sea level and presented no great problems to the early railway engineers or the later airfield builders.

All maps are to the scale of 25″ to 1 mile, unless otherwise stated.

HISTORICAL BACKGROUND

The first railway to Oxford was a branch from the Great Western Railway main line at Didcot and was opened on 12th June 1844. This was extended northward to Banbury in September 1850.

The London and North Western Railway arrived in Oxford in 1851, operating from Euston via Verney Junction and Bletchley.

The Oxford, Worcester and Wolverhampton Railway commenced operations at Oxford on 4th June 1853. It was with this distant railway network established that a group of Witney residents resolved to build their own local railway.

After over 20 years of dispute between the main line companies, the locally inspired branch came into use for passengers on 13th November 1861 and for goods on 1st March 1862. In 1860 the OWWR became part of the West Midland Railway and it was this company that agreed to operate the Witney branch, but only after the goods facilities had been improved.

The WMR was in turn absorbed by the GWR, on 1st August 1863. Thus the GWR came to operate the branch, retaining 50% of the receipts.

The East Gloucestershire Railway was formed in 1861 to link Witney with Cheltenham and thus form part of the main line network. Work started at Cheltenham in 1865 on the 50-mile route but a change of plan concentrated effort on the 14 miles at the east end, between Witney and Fairford. Long before the line was complete, the Witney Railway was declared bankrupt, in 1867. After years in receivership, it was purchased by the GWR in 1890.

In the meantime, the EGR had been opened to Fairford on 14th January 1873 and was operated by the GWR from the outset. A new station had been built at Witney for through services, the original terminus being retained for goods traffic. This company was even less successful financially than its neighbour and was similarly acquired by the GWR in 1890, never completing its Cheltenham link.

While the EGR and the Witney Railway both brought considerable benefit to the agricultural communities in respect of easier marketing of their products, it was the WR that reversed the decline in the main industry of Witney – blanket manufacture. Mills elsewhere had turned to steam power and by 1866 this became a reality in Witney, owing to the cheap transport of coal by rail. Similarly, the end product could be transported away more economically.

The branch served the needs of the district quietly for about seventy years until it quite suddenly became unexpectedly busy in World War II, as vast airfields were built in its vicinity. Construction materials, armaments, munitions and servicemen by the thousand were transported, reaching particularly high levels in 1943-45.

After the War competition from road transport caused a decline in traffic on the branch, which culminated in the loss of passenger services entirely and goods facilities west of Witney from 18th June 1962, the last public train running on 16th June. The remaining section to Witney was officially closed on 2nd November 1970, it having carried only full wagon loads since 1966.

ON AND AFTER THURSDAY, NOV. 14, 1861,

THE

WITNEY RAILWAY

WILL BE

OPENED

FOR PASSENGER TRAFFIC,

AND TRAINS WILL RUN AT THE FOLLOWING TIMES:

UP TRAINS.

DISTANCE FROM WITNEY.	STATIONS.	1 2 3 Class.	1 2 3 Class.	1 2 3 Class.	1 2 3 Class.	FARES FROM WITNEY.		
MILES.		A.M.	A.M.	P.M.	P.M.	1st Class.	2nd Class.	3rd Class.
	WITNEY . . .	8 15	11 0	4 50	7 35	s. d.	s. d.	s. d.
2¼	SOUTH LEIGH . .	8 22	11 7	4 57	7 42	0 7	0 5	0 4
4¾	EYNSHAM . .	8 30	11 15	5 5	7 50	1 0	0 9	0 6
8¼	YARNTON . .	8 40	11 25	5 15	8 0	1 10	1 4	0 11
11¾	OXFORD . . .	8 50	11 35	5 25	8 10	2 6	1 9	1 3

DOWN TRAINS.

DISTANCE FROM OXFORD.	STATIONS.	1 2 3 Class.	1 2 3 Class.	1 2 3 Class.	1 2 3 Class.	FARES FROM OXFORD.		
MILES.		A.M.	H.A.M.	P.M.	P.M.	1st Class.	2nd Class.	3rd Class.
	OXFORD . .	9 0	11 50	5 40	8 30	s. d.	s. d.	s. d.
3½	YARNTON . .	9 10	12 0	5 50	8 40	0 10	0 7	0 5
7	EYNSHAM . .	9 18	12 8	5 57	8 48	1 8	1 2	0 10
9	SOUTH LEIGH .	9 25	12 15	6 5	8 55	2 1	1 5	1 0½
11¾	WITNEY . .	9 35	12 25	6 15	9 5	2 6	1 9	1 3

A. C. SHERRIFF,

Worcester, November 8, 1861.   GENERAL MANAGER.

PASSENGER SERVICES

The initial service was one of four trains per day each way between Witney and Oxford. As the junction station at Yarnton did not open until 1863, all trains had to run through to Oxford and largely continued to do so after its opening. The basic frequency remained unchanged for around forty years.

By 1910, there were five journeys on weekdays and one on Sundays. This pattern was little altered until the end of World War II, although some additional trains ran as far as Witney or Carterton. For example, in 1938 there were five short workings plus an extra train on Saturdays.

The post-war years were one of boom in public transport, largely due to continued petrol rationing. 1948 was typical with six trains running through to Fairford and two to Carterton, with two to Fairford on Sundays.

A slow decline in frequency took place in the 1950s, with Sunday trains being withdrawn in 1951. The final timetable was similar to the initial one – four trains, weekdays only.

OXFORD

1. The first train arrived at the city on 12th June 1844 and ran on Brunel's impressive 7ft gauge track. The first station was a little to the south of the present site and continued to be used by passengers until 1st October 1852. The subsequent platforms were still gas lit when photographed in 1970. (R. Lingard)

→

The 1921 survey shows only part of the extensive sidings in use at that time. The LNWR lines are on the right of the map and cross over the river on a swing bridge as they are a few feet lower than those of the GWR. Note the separate engine sheds. The LNWR's Rewley Road terminus is now used by a tyre supplier.

2. Oxford became an important traffic centre for both freight and passengers. The former is well illustrated here. With the brake van still out of sight, 2–6–2T no. 5152 enters the station on the up through line. Mechanical signalling ceased on 13th October 1973, when a panel box was opened. (L. Waters)

3. Southern Region locomotives were an everyday sight at Oxford but a Midland Region "Royal Scot" was unusual. This is no. 46122 *Royal Ulster Rifleman*. The photograph is included to give an impression of the up platform and the track layout before the station was rebuilt in 1971-72. (L. Waters collection)

4. Fairford trains used the up and down bay platforms – only the up one now remains in use. The bridge in the foreground once carried the track to the down bay – now it gives road access to the carriage sidings. The train is the 17.43 extra to Bicester Town on 22nd September 1987. (V. Mitchell)

NORTH OF OXFORD

5. 2–4–0T no. 3583 passes under a minor roadway leading to Port Meadows, with five coaches from Fairford. The privately owned wagons date the photograph as prior to nationalisation in 1948. (R.H.G. Simpson)

Via Taunton?!

6. The same locomotive returns to Fairford passing the Oxford North goods yard. During World War II a connection between the GWR and the LMS was laid at this location, the yard closing in 1945. (R.H.G. Simpson)

7. "Dean Goods" no. 2579 coasts into Oxford with a train from Fairford which would run parallel to the former LNWR lines from Bletchley for nearly two miles. They are seen on the right of this picture. Rewley Road closed to passengers on 1st October 1951. (R.H.G. Simpson)

WOLVERCOT PLATFORM

8. The GWR opened this stopping place on 1st February 1908, the LNWR having opened nearby Wolvercote Halt (with an 'e'!) in 1906. This photograph, from about 1911, shows a steam railcar or railmotor hauling a horse box. Services were withdrawn on 1st January 1916. (L. Waters collection)

Mr. C.R. Gordon Stuart, an enthusiastic ticket specialist, comments on this unusual specimen –

The ticket is an Excursion Return from HAMMERSMITH (GW & Metropolitan Joint Station) to FAIRFORD via Westbourne Park Junction and the class is shown as "CLOSED CARRIAGE". Both from its design and the fact that no actual class is shown, it is clear that this ticket was printed in 1873, the year in which the East Gloucestershire line was opened throughout to Fairford. What is so remarkable about it is that it survived in issue until December 2nd 1933, when it was issued to me as a Long Period Excursion (or Summer Ticket) for the fare of 15/3d.

WOLVERCOT JUNCTION

9. An up train from Fairford approaches signals that control the junction between the line from Worcester (on which it is travelling) and the main line from Birmingham and Banbury. In the background is the embankment carrying the tracks between Yarnton and the former LNWR route to Bletchley. Until September 1863, OWWR trains reached Euston by this circuitous path. The connection was closed on 8th November 1965. (L. Waters)

GREAT WESTERN RAILWAY.
Ticket for a Bicycle, Perambulator, or Child's Mail Cart with Passenger at Owner's Risk
WITNEY TO
any G W. Station not exceeding 12 miles
CARRIAGE PAID 6d.
This Ticket must be given up on arrival
See other side

609   609

Gt Western Ry   Gt Western Ry
Bampton Oxon   Bampton Oxon
TO
OXFORD
via Yarnton
THIRD CLASS
2/0   Fare   2/0
Issued subject to the conditions & regulations set out in the Company's Time Tables Bills & Notices
Oxford   Oxford

745   745

11. The gothic style porch of the station house gave weather protection to passengers waiting for up trains, while those on the down platform had the benefit of an unusually styled canopy. The Fairford branch diverged to the left.
(LGRP Courtesy David & Charles)

YARNTON

10. Two views from the early years of this century show the spartan conditions that prevailed at this remote country junction. Looking towards Oxford, which was more than three miles distant, we see the junction signals for the Yarnton Loop line to the LNWR and a typical Victorian cast iron gentleman's toilet, on the left.
(LGRP Courtesy David & Charles)

12. The station house was demolished at an early date and this simple wooden building was erected on the up platform. There was no road access to the station, passengers reaching the village of about 300 inhabitants by means of a long unlit footpath close to the graveyard. (Lens of Sutton)

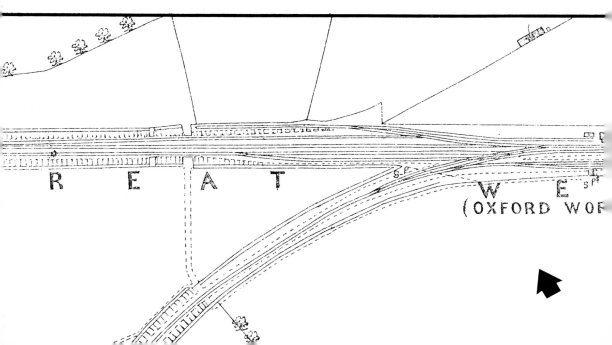

13. The down platform was built and used initially as an island platform but the loop line was fenced off later, as seen here. Evidence of decline is the missing portion of rainwater pipe above the letter box.
(Lens of Sutton)

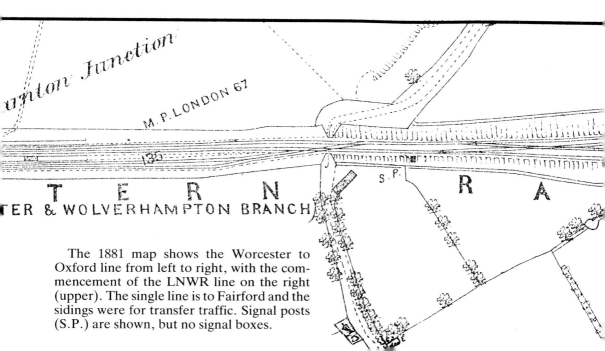

The 1881 map shows the Worcester to Oxford line from left to right, with the commencement of the LNWR line on the right (upper). The single line is to Fairford and the sidings were for transfer traffic. Signal posts (S.P.) are shown, but no signal boxes.

14. The McKenzie and Holland electric signal box came into use on 13th June 1909, replacing two boxes – Yarnton Witney Junction (at the down end of the down platform) and Yarnton Oxford Road Junction (close to the junction with the LNWR). Power at 120 volts was taken from two batteries of 60 cells each, which were charged by a 10HP oil engine, twice a week. The box was converted to orthodox working in February 1927. (Railway Engineer)

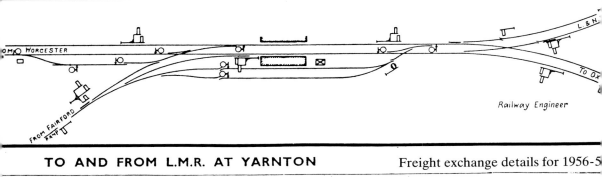

Railway Engineer

TO AND FROM L.M.R. AT YARNTON
Freight exchange details for 1956-5

Time Depart	From Yarnton to	Days run	Load	W.R. Feeding Service
1.15 a.m.	Saffron Lane Junction	Tuesdays to Saturdays	Empties	—
1.15 a.m.	Fletton's Siding	Sundays	Empties	—
2.50 a.m.	Blisworth	Sundays	Empties	3. 5 p.m. Rogerstone (SO).
3. 0 a.m.	Irthlingboro'	Tuesday to Saturdays	Empties	3. 5 p.m. Rogerstone.
6.25 a.m.	Corby	Monday	Goods	—
7.55 a.m.	Swanbourne	Weekdays	Goods	7.40 p.m. Pontypool Road
10.15 a.m.	Swanbourne	Weekdays	Goods	—
11. 0 a.m.	Cambridge	Mondays to Saturdays	Goods	2.45 p.m. Severn Tunnel Jn.
7.45 p.m.	Swanbourne	Weekdays	Empties	—
9.30 p.m.	Northampton	Saturdays	Goods	5.10 a.m. Pontypool Road
10.50 p.m.	Northampton	Mondays to Fridays	Goods	5.10 a.m. Pontypool Road
11.45 p.m.	Cambridge	Mondays to Saturdays	Goods	12.10 p.m. Llandilo Jn.

Train		Time Due	Days Run	W.R. Connection Yarnton to
Time	From			
9.45 a.m.	Cambridge SX	1.45 p.m.	Mondays to Fridays	3.35 p.m. Cardiff
9.45 a.m.	Cambridge SO	1.45 p.m.	Saturdays	8.40 p.m. Honeybourne
7.42 a.m.	Wellingboro'	4. 0 p.m.	Mondays to Saturdays	4.35 p.m. Honeybourne
11.40 a.m.	Irthlingboro'	5. 0 p.m.	Tuesdays, Fridays and Saturdays	8.40 p.m. Honeybourne
4 0 p.m.	Bletchley MO	5.23 p.m.	Mondays	—
12.45 p.m.	Irthlingboro'	5.25 p.m.	Wednesdays and Thursdays	8.40 p.m. Honeybourne.
2. 0 p.m.	Irthlingboro'	7.20 p.m.	Mondays to Saturdays	11.55 p.m. Honeybourne

15. A typical Western Region branch train with an ex-GWR 0-6-0 pannier tank nears the end of the single line, as it passes the junction signals and the rhubarb of a local railwayman's lineside allotment. (B. Robinson)

16. To facilitate the handling of the heavy military traffic in WWII, nine exchange sidings and a turntable were laid down on the south side of the branch. They were brought into use on 20th August 1940 for the remarshalling of freight between the GWR and LMS, and were later used for ironstone traffic, eventually being closed on 6th July 1966. (R.H.G. Simpson)

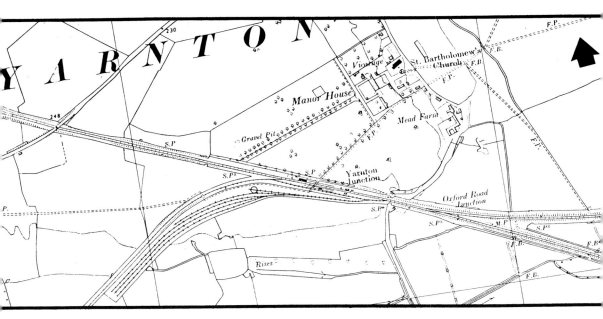

The scale of 6″ to 1 mile is required to give an impression of the extent of the exchange sidings.

17. 0–6–0PT no. 9773 hauls a train of Southern Region coaches forming a Locomotive Club of Great Britain railtour to the branch, on 25th July 1965. The main line up home signal is in the background. (R.H.G. Simpson)

18. The signal box closed on 28th March 1971 but had been boarded up previously, as this February 1970 photograph shows. One hinged panel is visible. This gave Mr. Hawtin, the last signalman, visibility and daylight. (R. Lingard)

19. On 23rd September 1987, the 8.08 Hereford to Oxford passes the turntable pit, the only remaining relic of this once extensive junction. Even the main line is now only single track, the up line having been taken out of use on 29th November 1971. (V. Mitchell)

CASSINGTON

20. The penultimate stopping place to open on the branch, this halt came into use on 9th March 1936, at a site on the south side of the A40. This view is of the second platform, on the north side of the road and railway. In the early 1930s, a new main road was built to pass north of Oxford, south of Cassington and north of Eynsham. This is now the busy A40 trunk road and was carried over the railway on this traditional Cotswold stone bridge. (Lens of Sutton)

21. The single concrete platform served about 300 villagers, who had direct access to the halt by means of a private lane. The danger of crossing the A40 is the reason given for moving the platform after WWII. 0–6–0PT no. 9640 passes through with a freight service from Oxford on 19th May 1959. It will shortly pass over the Evenlode Viaduct and the short Cassington Canal. Noteworthy are the brick steps used by the guard to tend the oil lamps. (M. Hale)

22. Half a mile before reaching Eynsham, a depot was to be seen on the south side of the line. Sidings were provided here between 1927 and 1929 for Sugar Beet & Crop Driers Ltd. These sidings reopened in 1936. During WWII they were used by the Royal Army Service Corp and later by the NAAFI. This Brush 0–4–0ST shunted the sidings initially and was photographed in 1949, in new ownership. (F. Jones/Leicester Museum)

EYNSHAM

23. The Witney Railway's timber building here shows many similar features to its terminal station at Witney, while the 1890s signal box is similar to its counterpart at Fairford. A generous manning level was provided for a town of 2000 people. (Lens of Sutton)

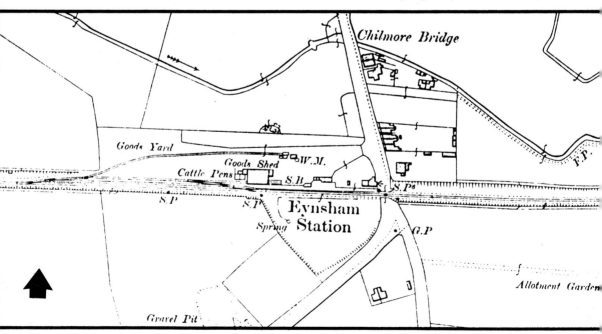

The 1913 edition shows the additional siding, north of the goods shed, laid in 1878 to handle the increasing traffic in domestic coal.

25. Work is seen in progress in May 1944 on the preparation of the track bed for a passing loop. This was required in order to increase the single capacity for troop and material movements needed for the invasion of Europe. (British Rail)

24. The goods shed was also similar to its companion at Witney, but was closer to the passenger platform. The close proximity of the signals is a remarkable feature.
(British Rail)

26. A lens on the original photograph reveals a GWR railcar approaching. These cars were used on the Oxford - Thame services and in the 1950s one of them made one return trip to Fairford in the early morning. The children are standing on the timbered area once used for the transfer of milk churns. (British Rail)

28. The two houses are the only buildings still standing, although the goods shed survived for many years as a scenery workshop for the Oxford Playhouse. The spare screw coupling on the goods shed wall was photographed on 14th May 1951. (R.C. Riley)

27. Milk churns appear in this picture, although ironically awaiting transport by road. They are standing on the site of a new traffic roundabout and became historic exhibits themselves in August 1978, when the Milk Marketing Board changed to bulk tanker collection. (British Rail)

29. The station building was extended in 1878 – the narrower boarding is evident in this view. The concrete lamp posts were replaced by ones with concrete brackets (compare with the previous picture) but the pressurised oil lamps were still hoisted up on a wire. (Lens of Sutton)

31. The signalman prepares to exchange the single line token before returning to his 1892 signal box which was adorned, like others on the line, with a horseshoe for luck. The 1944 sectional platform has been rebuilt at the Great Western Society's Didcot Railway Centre. (M. Hale)

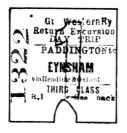

Gt Western Ry
Return Excursion
DAY TRIP
PADDINGTON to
EYNSHAM
via Reading & Oxford
THIRD CLASS
R.I

30. During the period of post-war austerity, the close-boarded goods shed doors were replaced by the draughty type, seen here. No. 9654 accelerates towards Fairford, past the sidings at which wagons loaded with animal bones once stood, prior to cartage to the glue works at Eynsham Mill. (T. Wright)

32. Photographed in 1961, no. 9654 drifts over the level crossing which, was substantially rearranged in 1944. The trap points on the left were laid at that time and led to a short siding for some while. (T. Wright)

33. A 1970 picture shows the lean-to extension in which the ladies room was earlier situated. The new route of the B4044 is along the track bed. An interesting piece of transport history is perpetuated on this road, a mile westwards, where it crosses the River Thames on a toll bridge. The fee for a car is 2p! (R. Lingard)

34. The down platform and the goods shed were still obvious from the new road in 1983. A roundabout now exists at this road junction and the only station in the vicinity is the fire station. (R. Lingard)

SOUTH LEIGH

35. The rustic scene is enhanced by an all-wood platform seat. These were replaced in the early years of this century by ones with cast iron ends containing the letters GWR. The East Ground Frame can be seen – the other one was at the far end of the loop. (LGRP Courtesy David & Charles)

36. Beyond the small cattle dock, the extensive buildings of a WWII buffer food store are visible. The goods loop was extended as a private siding in 1942 to serve this depot. Note the unusual free standing brick chimney which was linked to the stove under the window. Like the toilets, it was an afterthought. (Lens of Sutton)

37. The porter waits at the crossing hut as the freight from Oxford arrives on 19th May 1959. The outbuildings housed the toilets – late additions to the railway scene and not originally deemed necessary by the "penny-pinching" directors of the Witney Railway. (M. Hale)

Gt. Western Ry		Gt. Western Ry
Witney		Witney
042	**SOUTH LEIGH** TO THIRD CLASS 5d N Fare 5d N Issued subject to the conditions&regulations set out in theCompanys Time Tables Bills&Notices	042
	South Leigh South Leigh	

38. An eastward view from the goods yard shows the crossing keeper's cottage in the distance and the parcels shed which also had doors opening onto the pasenger platform. The siding was closed in April 1964. (S.C. Jenkins)

The 1st edition of Ordnance Survey indicates a short goods loop. Apart from this being lengthened, no changes occurred throughout the life of the station.

39. Many larger goods yards did not have the luxury of a weighbridge. This hut housed the weighing machine and was fitted with a hinged panel which could be dropped down for viewing. The thatched roofs of Station Farm are visible. (S.C. Jenkins)

→

40. By 1970 the crossing gate had been abandoned against the wall of the cottage and replaced by rope. The 300 local residents were left remote from main roads and an adequate bus service. (R. Lingard)

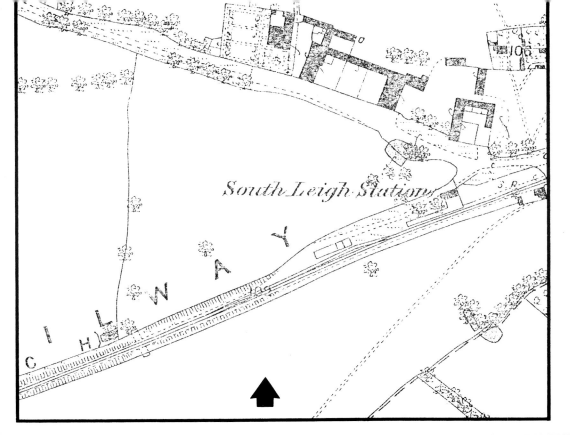

South Leigh Station

C I H L W A Y

41. A porter met all freight trains having work to do in the yard at Witney at the Junction Ground Frame, where he would obtain the electric train tablet from the engineman and work the necessary points to admit the engine into the yard. When the train was clear of the points in the goods line, he would take the tablet to the station signal box where it was placed into the slide and the section from Witney to Eynsham cleared. When it was necessary for a train to leave Witney goods yard, the porter obtained a tablet from the Witney signalman, took it to the Junction Ground Frame and operated the points, allowing the train to leave the yard before handing the tablet to the driver. When the train was ready to leave the yard, the engineman blew one crow on the whistle to summon the porter and to indicate to the signalman that he was ready to leave. In this view, the wagon labels are being checked. A signal box was erected here in 1892 but had only a short life. (LGRP Courtesy of David & Charles)

42. Officially described as a velocipede car, this machine was fitted with two pairs of handles to give high and low "gear" and clips on the outrigger for spanner and hammer. The track has inside keys, a feature still to be seen in the siding at Hampton Loade, on the Severn Valley Railway. (British Rail)

2nd- SINGLE SINGLE -2nd

South Leigh to

South Leigh   South Leigh
Witney   Witney

WITNEY

(W)   8d. Fare 8d.   (W)

8235   8235

43. The Locomotive Club of Great Britain celebrated its 21st anniversary by running "The Isis" railtour on 14th February 1970, which originated at Bath Spa and included the Witney and Wallingford branches. The train became entangled in the telephone wire seen in front of it. (I.K. Mowles)

The 1921 survey shows the relationship between the WR terminus and the later EGR station. The road past the new station had been built in 1860-61, for the benefit of the residents of Ducklington, a village to the south.

WITNEY GOODS

45. The fame of Witney blankets was partly due to good publicity, which was the purpose of this photograph. Even no. 1249, an outside framed "Buffalo" with partial cab, bears a poster proclaiming that Witney blankets cover the world! (British Rail)

44. Following the extension of the railway from Witney to Fairford in 1873, the original terminus became a goods depot, the principal merchandise to be despatched being the blankets for which the town is famed worldwide. 2–2–2 no. 1124 of the "Sir Alexander" class stands at the head of a blanket special in 1911. (S.C. Jenkins collection)

46. No opportunity was lost to advertise as the consignment left Paddington Goods Station for delivery to the well known London shop. Witney's declining blanket industry made a remarkable recovery with the advent of a railway to the town. (British Rail)

WITNEY BLANKETS
SPECIAL TRAIN LOAD
MAPLE'S

WITNEY BLANKETS
SPECIAL TRAIN LOAD
FOR
MAPLE'S

GREAT WESTERN RAILWAY 489

GREAT WESTERN RAILWAY

47. Station Master Pugh sits with his clerical staff, while the other ranks stand behind. The goods and passenger stations had a combined staff of 12 in 1886, increasing to 24 by 1905. (S.C. Jenkins collection)

48. Originally an almost square building (as at South Leigh), the building was extended on each side and provided with chimneys (as at Eynsham). After the cessation of passenger services in 1873, the platform area under the canopy was boarded in, to increase parcel storage space. Until about 1900, a locomotive shed stood at the end of the line – only its water tank remains at the end of the platform in this 1933 view. (LGRP Courtesy David & Charles)

49. One of Marriott's wooden coal wagons appears in the previous photograph. This all steel double door version was completed in November 1933. The family continue to retail coal from the now rail-less yard.
(British Rail)

50. The substantial stone goods shed was erected by the WR in response to a demand by the WMR who operated the line. It was later extended in timber as a result of increased traffic. No. 9640 shunts the shed road on 19th May 1959. The spire of St. Mary's Church marks the southern border of the town.
(M. Hale)

51. In addition to the goods shed, there was a corrugated iron warehouse (often used by Bibbys for storage of seed potatoes and grain) and a stable block for dray horses, which were sometimes used for shunting wagons. No. D6348 carries out this function on a dismal January day in 1968, the last steam working having been on the last day of 1965. (S.C. Jenkins)

52. Believed to be the last station master's house erected by the GWR, this dwelling commanded an excellent view of the goods yard, as is apparent in photograph no.50. This and the next two pictures were taken in September 1987. (V. Mitchell)

53. Most of the former railway land is now in commercial use but the former goods shed has been converted into a club, access being through a 1955 ex-BR MkI coach. The weighbridge and its brick-built machine house survive redevelopment. (V. Mitchell)

54. The northern chimney stack was accidentally felled in 1980 when a tractor-mounted loading shovel became entangled in an electric cable that was attached to it. Marriott's contemporary transport has become a potential historic exhibit, as Bedford lorries are no longer produced. (V. Mitchell)

WITNEY

55. A postcard of indifferent quality is included because it shows an unusual and illogical feature, namely the water column *beyond* the down starting signal. Locomotives would have to wait for the arrival of a passing up train before being able to take water. (Lens of Sutton)

56. A detail of interest in this view is the complex passenger and barrow crossing. Such timbers seemed to have a particular affinity for frost and this, combined with the irregular slopes nearby, would cause problems for a porter with a heavily laden barrow. (British Rail)

57. No. 7411 clatters over the points as it arrives from Fairford on 4th May 1951, with tablet hoop projecting. It appears that the inside keyed track was about to be replaced. (R.C. Riley)

58. A view from the bridge helps to emphasise the squat, tough appearance of the EGR's stone-built stations, contrasting markedly with the WR's timber affairs. While bulk consignments of blankets were despatched by goods trains, small batches were sent by passenger train, as witnessed here. (R. Lingard collection)

59. Collett 0–6–0 no. 2221 arrives from Fairford "wrong road", as vans stood in the up platform all day in the early 1960s. They arrived at the goods station in the 5.45 am freight from Oxford and were then propelled into this platform where they stood until 7.10 pm. (T. Wright)

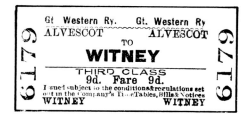

60. Another westward view shows the revised position for the water column – the signal is just visible, beyond it. The platforms were necessarily extended eastwards – the change from coping slabs to chequered bricks is evident. (British Rail)

61. On the left is the original stone abutment that was retained when a new and longer steel span was installed. Compare the bridges in pictures 55 and 60. The dock on the right gave end and side loading facilities. (British Rail)

62. The locomotive water tank and the permanent way hut were situated opposite the dock. A pump trolley stands outside the hut in the previous photograph. Note the level indicator weight, which was simply attached to a float by means of a rope. The building housed a pump which raised the water from a well. (British Rail)

63. The position of the station clock and the gentlemen's toilet are revealed in this 1957 photograph. The white painted corner of the signal box was a legacy of the wartime days of blackout. (R.M. Casserley)

64. The pagoda was a typical GWR feature, being erected as passenger shelters or parcel sheds, with lockable doors. Its roof finials complement the well ornamented gas lamps. The signalman and driver stand by the

brazier which was lit in deep winter to pre-
vent the water column freezing. The photograph was taken on 2nd February 1957.
(R.M. Casserley)

65. An end opening van stands in the up
platform as the 1.10 pm from Fairford arrives
behind no. 9611 on 19th May 1959. A van
leads the formation, confirming the extent of

parcel traffic on the branch, particularly at
Witney. Further confirmation is to be seen at
the end of the platform. (M. Hale)

66. 0–6–0 no. 2236 negotiates the chicane as it leaves for Fairford on 25th April 1957, while the exhaust of another locomotive rises from the goods yard. Trunks are in evidence, as another term at boarding school began for some, another reminder of a former railway traffic. (British Rail)

67. A shabby no. 7445 has its tanks replenished as the shadows lengthen on the platform and on the future of the branch. The signal gives an emphatic deep nod to show that all is still well, but the fireman seems deep in thought in this peaceful scene. (L. Waters)

68. Only four months before the end of passenger services, an even dirtier pannier tank, no. 9654 waits with the 2.25 pm Fairford to Oxford service. An air of despondency had settled over the winter railway scene, as steam issued from places it should not.
(R. Lingard collection)

BRIZE NORTON &
BAMPTON

69. A trainless view gives us the opportunity to appreciate the length of the loop (at least one 16-coach train ran in wartime) and also to see through the goods shed. Few stations were provided with two foot crossings. (British Rail)

70. The name was changed from Bampton (Oxon) in May 1940 to end confusion with Bampton in Devon and to recognise that the RAF Brize Norton Airfield existed nearby. For over 50 years, this station had the only other passing loop on the line. The living van in this 1956 view probably accompanied a steam roller. (H.C. Casserley)

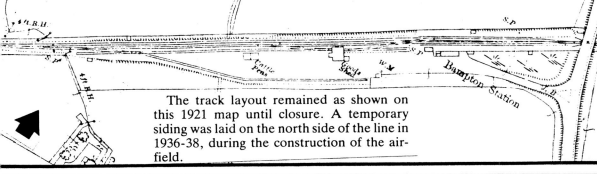

The track layout remained as shown on this 1921 map until closure. A temporary siding was laid on the north side of the line in 1936-38, during the construction of the airfield.

71. No. 9611 on the 1.00 pm from Fairford crosses no. 9653 with the 12.58 pm from Oxford on 16th May 1959. The signal box was linked to the RAF control tower, as part of the camp was south of the line and aircraft had to taxi across it. The beautiful ridge of the Cotswolds can be seen to the right of the inelegant hangar. (M. Hale)

72. Bampton has been described as a decayed market town, its population falling from 1400 in 1881 to 1200 in 1901. Being two miles south of the station, it did not benefit greatly from the arrival of the railway. The goods shed was almost identical to the others erected by the EGR. Most contained a 30 cwt. crane and were devoid of dressed quoins.
(S.C. Jenkins)

CARTERTON

73. The austere station was opened hurriedly during the invasion of Europe in 1944. The loop came into use on 10th August and the platforms in October. This photograph, dated 11th November, is marked "progress". No nameboards were displayed during the war. It served RAF Broadwell and the west end of RAF Brize Norton, two of ten such establishments close to the branch at this time. (British Rail)

74. A 1961 picture shows a train approaching from Fairford. William Carter established a number of smallholdings in the area, prior to WWI. These later generated a small amount of rail traffic in such commodities as mushrooms and tomatoes, which were carried by passenger train. (T. Wright)

75. Being a latecomer, the signal box was unlike the others on the branch. Black Bourton was the first name proposed for the station. This was only ½ mile to the south whereas Carterton was a mile north, on the far side of the airfield. To reach it by road, it was necessary to pass Alvescot station! Ben Davies shows that bored signalman enjoyed a variety of rural activities. (B. Davies)

76. To minimise earthworks on overbridge approaches, the line was dipped steeply, as seen here as the 1.09 pm arrives from Fairford, behind no. 3653 on 26th May 1962. Remarkably, no public roads passed under the 22-mile long branch. (M. Hale)

77. The signalman's allotment seems in good order while weeds grow in profusion on the track. No. 7445 waits in the down platform as no. 9654 leaves for Oxford. No sidings were provided at this station. (T. Wright)

ALVESCOT

78. The station served a community of about 300 people, the centre of the village being less than ½-mile to the north. 0–6–0 no. 2236 darkens the sky as it departs for Oxford with the afternoon freight on a gloomy day in February 1957. (R.M. Casserley)

79. Goods facilities comprised a loop ending at the dock by the goods shed and a single siding passing by the coal staithes on the left. Although of similar design to the EGR station, this one was built of brick instead of stone. The yard is still occupied by a coal merchant (G.F. Luckett) but the buildings have been demolished. (British Rail)

KELMSCOT & LANGFORD

80. Situated in a flat, almost treeless, landscape the platform was brought into use on 4th November 1907, the single siding not being available for traffic until 9th July 1928. It was in an isolated location, ½-mile south of Langford (pop. 300) and 1½ miles north of Kelmscot (pop. 100). Look for the "Lifebuoy" Tilley lamp. (British Rail)

81. It was the only *station* on the branch to be opened in peacetime by the GWR and was composed entirely of their standard corrugated iron clad structures. The main building was two pagodas erected end to end – probably the longest building of this type anywhere. (Lens of Sutton)

82. In September 1987, more remained of this station than most – two lamp posts, two nameboard posts and the platform edge. General goods had not been handled here – only full wagon loads. (V. Mitchell)

83. Shortly before crossing the county boundary into Gloucestershire, the line crossed the lane to Little Faringdon. Such crossings were normally protected by distant signals, but all such signals had been removed from the branch and replaced by a locomotive-mounted audible warning system, as part of experiments which led the GWR to introduce automatic train control. Thus the levers in the small cabin, photographed in 1981, only operated electromagnetic ramps between the rails. (R. Lingard)

LECHLADE

84. With a staff of only six, the station served a town of about 1200 people, ½-mile to the south, and in some years handled over 10,000 tons of goods. Shunting is in progress in 1921, apparently by one of the "Buffalo" class. (LGRP Courtesy David & Charles)

85. Privately owned wagons are again part of the railway scene, after a long absence following nationalisation. With fleet no. 11, this fine example of the wagon builder's craft is worthy of detailed study. (British Rail)

The only addition to the 1921 layout, seen here, was a siding near to the southern boundary fence, brought into use in July 1940 as part of the war effort.

86. The 1935 allocation from the Road Transport Department was Thornycroft no. 3009 and trailer no. T340. The horn projects to the left of the radiator – its rubber bulb was situated inside the cab. (British Rail)

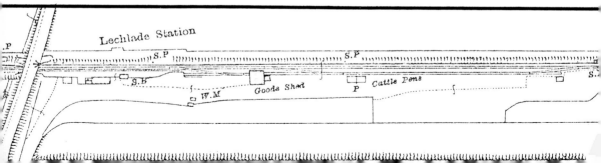

87. Although the goods yard contained a loop from earliest times, it was not until October 1944 that it was signalled for use by passing trains, but then only for one goods and one passenger or two goods. This photograph was taken in February 1957. (R.M. Casserley)

88. A fine topiary hen looks over the fence at the exceptionally well laid out garden and two passengers, a rare feature of photographs of the branch. The loop had been substantially lengthened at the far end, in 1944. (British Rail)

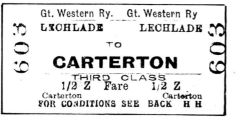

603   603

| Gt. Western Ry. | Gt. Western Ry |
| LECHLADE | LECHLADE |

TO

CARTERTON

THIRD CLASS
1/2 Z   Fare   1/2 Z
Carterton   Carterton
FOR CONDITIONS SEE BACK H H

89. Three more rarities and a horseshoe appear in this photograph which is of interest because it shows flooding under the bridge. All the economical dips were thus prone and caused problems with instability of the track bed. (British Rail)

90. All eyes are on the solitary lady shuffling towards the open carriage door. There is time enough for the signalman and fireman to enjoy a chat and for the young cyclist to enjoy looking at another train. Alas only the chequered paving bricks remain from this peaceful scene of May 1959. (M. Hale)

91. A view from the road bridge shows the typical roof-less gentlemen's toilet, horse boxes in the 1940 siding and a ring on the goods loop signal, a feature not seen in earlier pictures. Assorted parcels are under discussion in this 1961 photograph.
(T. Wright)

92. Soon after closure, motor vehicles invaded the yard, after having been responsible for the death of the line. Examples from the leading manufacturers of the day stand on the former cattle dock. From left to right — Vauxhall, Ford, Austin and Hillman.
(British Rail)

FAIRFORD (GWR)

93. Fairford was the optimistic name given to the terminus which was over a mile from the town centre. The land westwards slopes down to the River Coln, so that further extension of the line would have involved expensive civil engineering. This is believed to be the scene on the opening day, 15th January 1873. The locomotive appears to be an 0–4–2ST of the 517 class, the members of which were built at Wolverhampton between 1868 and 1885. (Railway Magazine)

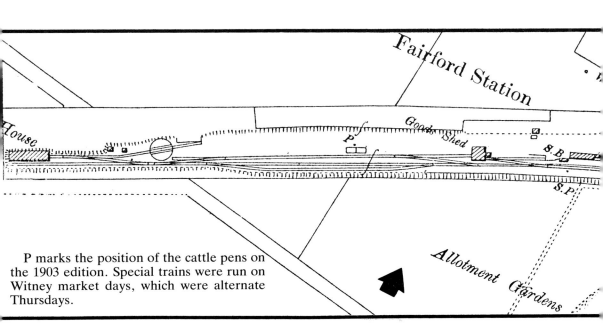

P marks the position of the cattle pens on the 1903 edition. Special trains were run on Witney market days, which were alternate Thursdays.

94. A typical view from the road bridge between the wars shows clerestory coaches and a "Metro" tank, with shunting in progress in the yard.
(LGRP Courtesy David & Charles)

→

96. The change in coping stones indicates the end of the original short platform. The track in this and the two previous pictures can be seen to be the early inside keyed type. The purpose of the well secured trunk is a mystery. (British Rail)

95. Five photographs from January 1932 record in detail the good order in which the station was kept at that time. The signal controlled entry to the goods yard. (British Rail)

97. Three types of barrow are on display, as is a reminder that beer was carried by the GWR from as far away as London. The coming of the railway killed off many local breweries. (British Rail)

98. The unusual pentagonal signal box is evident here. Had it been rectangular, the corner nearest the end loading dock would have restricted access to it. Milk to London was an important traffic on the branch, over 15,000 gallons *per day* being carried for many years. (British Rail)

99. As at the other principal stations, the toilets were an afterthought and were housed in the extension on the left. The horse box indicates the position of the end/side loading dock. (British Rail)

100. American servicemen unload coal and local woodmen load timber as the ground is excavated, in 1944, in readiness for a new siding to be laid. It branched off the goods shed road, a little to the west of the building. The cattle pen had disappeared by then. (British Rail)

FAIRFORD (BR) –
The Station

→

102. The 1400 class 0–4–2Ts were a common sight on other Western Region branches, but generally only appeared at Fairford when the pannier tanks were being serviced. The crew rest by the signal box – they were one of four sets of men based at Fairford. This locomotive is now preserved on the Dart Valley Railway at Buckfastleigh. (Lens of Sutton)

101. Pre-war photographs show oil lamp hoists of the type seen at the other stations on the branch, but here we see that the lighting has been "modernised" with gas. The initials GWR are more easily seen in the seat castings in this view. (J. Russell)

→

103. Empty trains ran forward onto the loop in the distance where the locomotive would run round. We have no record of push-pull working rendering this movement unnecessary. Note the unusual roof profile at this end of the signal box. (British Rail)

104. The neatly pitched roof at this end gives a false impression of the signal box width. The boxes are a reminder that railways carried horticultural produce, such as cabbages and cauliflowers, in large quantities, particularly to London. (R.C. Riley)

105. The signal is "off" for no. 4676 to proceed to the yard for turning and watering as a passenger makes his way towards the Austin A30. Passengers were never prolific here, as the town had only about 1400 inhabitants. (J. Russell)

106. A dull day in February 1957 adds to the melancholy of the approach to the deserted terminus, surrounded by empty fields. At least a gas lamp was provided for the benefit of the late traveller on foot. (R.M. Casserley)

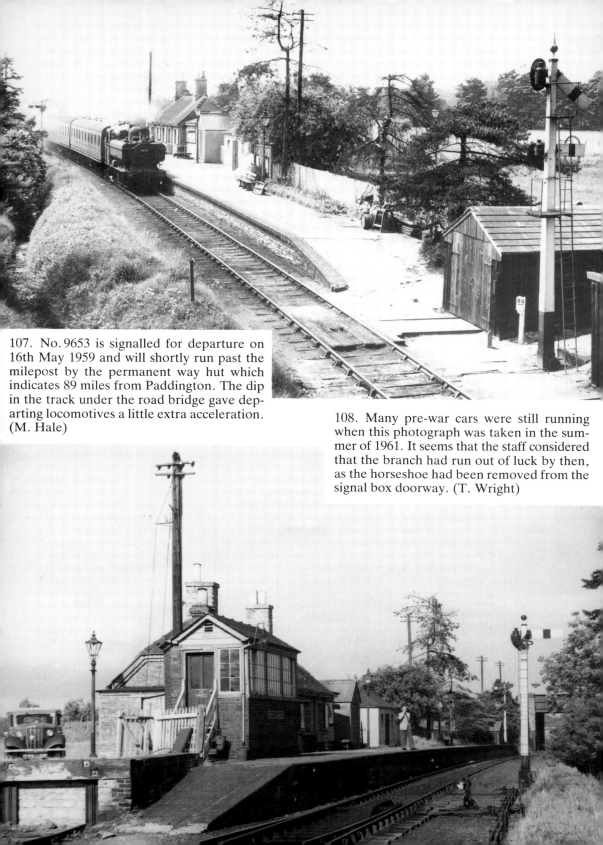

107. No. 9653 is signalled for departure on 16th May 1959 and will shortly run past the milepost by the permanent way hut which indicates 89 miles from Paddington. The dip in the track under the road bridge gave departing locomotives a little extra acceleration. (M. Hale)

108. Many pre-war cars were still running when this photograph was taken in the summer of 1961. It seems that the staff considered that the branch had run out of luck by then, as the horseshoe had been removed from the signal box doorway. (T. Wright)

FAIRFORD (BR) –
The Yard

109. A pannier tank is partly in view on the 1944 siding. Also to be seen are a Vulcan lorry and the shunt signal that controlled the departure from the yard. There is one loading gauge above the wagons and one in the shed. (British Rail)

110.   The 6-ton capacity crane is visible in the yard as no. 7436 takes water on 14th May 1951. Water was raised from a well by means of steam supplied from locomotive injectors, a number of tank engines being specially adapted for this purpose. (R.C. Riley)

111. The end of the branch, as seen on 16th May 1959 as no. 9653 took water and no. 2252 simmered quietly. This branch line enthusiast's dream came to an end without the intervention of full dieselisation. (M. Hale)

112. Steam is raised on no. 7436 in May 1951, outside the 1872 locomotive shed which could only accommodate two *tank* engines, as it was only 90ft. long. A redundant horse box body was provided as a mess room. (R.C. Riley)

→

113. The 45ft. turntable was photographed on 27th May 1961. The fireman holds the locking lever while behind him is the winding mechanism, which was later removed. (P. Hay)

→

114. Following the removal of the gearing, the turntable had to be laboriously turned by muscle power, as witnessed here. An antifreeze brazier stands idle under the 5000 gallon tank. (British Rail)

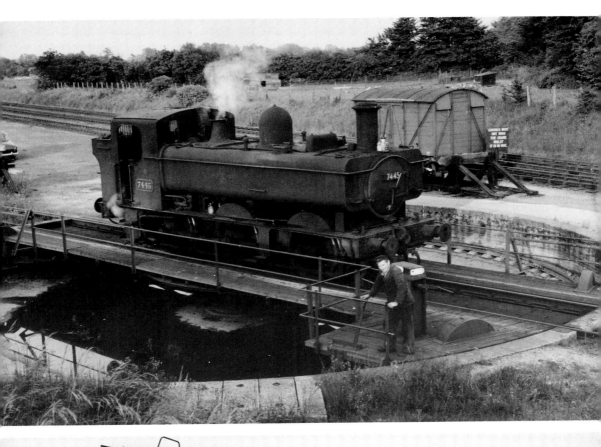

FAIRFORD – The closure

115. The 6.49 pm from Oxford on Saturday 16th June 1962, the last day of public passenger services, carried the Oxford University Railway Society's headboard, as members were making a farewell trip on the train. (R.H.G. Simpson)

→

117. Having stood for nearly 100 years, the shed was not fit for re-use. It is thought that the design originated from the days of the GWR's broad gauge. The notice refers to the danger of crawling on the fragile asbestos roof covering. (S.J. Dickson)

ENGINES MUST
NOT PASS
THE CRANE
WHILST
IT IS IN USE

116. After cessation of services, weeds quickly took control and all notices became meaningless. Thomas Ward & Co started to lift the track in late 1964, taking the materials to Lechlade from where pannier tanks collected train loads twice a week. (S.J. Dickson)

118. The structures became vandalised and
even the ground signal was uprooted and
turned round. Road improvements eventually led to the removal of the bridge and
approach ramps. None of the 13 levers in the
signal box would ever be used again.
(S.J. Dickson)

OXFORD, WITNEY AND FAIRFORD.

			Week Days.															Sundays.	
Miles.			a.m.	a.m.	a.m.		a.m.		p.m.	p.m.	p.m.		p.m.	p.m.	p.m.		p.m.		p.m.		p.m.		p.m.	
	Oxford . . . . dep.	7 32	7 57	9 20	..	11 50	..	12 20	1 15		3 25	3 42	4 22	..	6 15	..	9 35	..	11 0	..		5 10	..
3¾	Yarnton . . . . ,,	7 40	8 5	9 28	..	11 58	..	12 28	1 23		3 33	3 50	4 30	..	6 23	..	9 43	..	11 8	..		5 23	..
7¼	Eynsham . . . . . . ,,		8 12	9 35	..	12 5	..	12 35			3 40		4 37	..	6 30	..	9 50	..	11 15	..		5 23	..
9¼	South Leigh . . . . . . ,,		8 18	9 41	..	12 11	..	12 41			3 46		4 43	..	6 36	..	9 56	..	11 21	..		5 29	..
12	**Witney** . . . . . . { arr.		8 23	9 46	..	12 16	..	12 46			3 51		4 48	..	6 41	..	10 1	..	11 26	..		5 34	..
	{ dep.		8 25	9 49	..	12 19	..				3 54		4 52	..	6 49	..	10 4	..				5 37	..
15¾	Bampton (Oxon) . . . . ,,		8 35	9 57	..	12 27					4 1		5 0	..	6 55	..	10 12	..				5 45	..
17¾	Alvescot . . . . . . ,,		..	10 4	..	12 33		Sats. only.	Thurs. and Sats. only.		..		5 5	..	7 4	..	10 15	..		Sats. only.		5 51	..
20¼	Kelmscott and Langford . . ,,		..	10 10	..	12 39					..		5 11	..	7 11	..	10 27	..				..	..
22¼	Lechlade . . . . . . ,,		..	10 18	..	12 45					..		5 17	..	7 18	..	10 34	..				6 3	..
25¾	**Fairford** . . . . arr.		..	10 24	..	12 51					..		5 23	..	7 24	..	10 40	..				6 9	..

1934

119. The signalling had been modernised at most of the stations but here the tapered wooden posts remained to the end, together with S on the shunt signal instead of a circle. (S.J. Dickson)

120. Years after closure, the buildings were adapted as offices. The doorway to the platform was blocked up, the chimney stacks removed and the toilet block extended. Antocks Lairn Ltd., manufacturers of office chairs, are now responsible for the survival of this interesting relic of a much loved era of local transport. (V. Mitchell)